T0366037

HOCKEY ON THE ROOF?

Written By: SHERRY PAULINO

Illustrated By:
SHERRY PAULINO
and
CARLI TAYLOR

To order additional copies of this book, contact:
Xlibris
844-714-8691
www.Xlibris.com
Orders@Xlibris.com

ISBN: Softcover   978-1-4257-7030-3

Print information available on the last page

Rev. date: 04/15/2024

Dedicated To:
CARLI TAYLOR and my MOTHER, who helped inspire me to write this childrens' book.

Far away in a little town just above Paradise lives a wonderful family of three. They live beautiful, splendid lives with birds chirping, deer wandering, squirrels playing and nearly every animal you can think of playing while the family watches out their windows while drinking their morning coffee.

Grandma sits on her front porch occasionally playing solitaire as the beautiful deer wander by, stop to eat her precious flowers and then go lay on her manicured lawn for a long nap after their feast.

Grandma's daughter Sherry goes out to the porch to keep Grandma company and sees two cute little squirrels, Josh and Gosh, playing and running around the acorn tree out front.

Wait a minute ... these two characters are dropping acorns on each other as they're playing and I believe Josh has a Mohawk down the center of his head?!! Oh my, Grandma, these two look like trouble!

The bluejays are quietly grabbing peanuts from the squirrels and hiding them in Grandma's planter boxes on the porch. One bluejay, Mac, is so different that he's burying his peanuts in the plastic plants with no dirt in them, But he's happy as a lark because he's hiding his peanuts in his special hiding place.

Oh, here come the tedious dog walkers with their studious pets dressed for the occasion in their best dressed coats.

And they're sooo good at bringing home their pet's treasures. This keeps Grandma's neighborhood sooo clean.

Well, time for Grandma and Sherry to go inside and put on a giant pot of spaghetti for everyone's dinner. A little garlic bread will go nicely.

The deer are ready to get up from their long nap and move on.
What's this?!! The beautiful manicured lawn peeled right up with the deer
and stayed right on their sides!! Grandma is going to be very mad when
she sees her lawn walking away on four legs.

Well, the mail lady is here today. Sherry says, "I'll go get the mail, Grandma." Sherry steps
down the front steps of the porch and hollers, "GRANDMA! Come out here, quick!"

Grandma puts the cover on the spaghetti, runs outside, and ... and ... she blows her top!
Her beautiful lawn is walking away and she sees it has four feet below it!
Oh, what is Grandma to do!

Oh no, Grandma better run inside and stir the boiling
spaghetti sauce before it boils over.

Well, it's just about time for Carli to get home from school. She runs inside
and goes straight to Buttons the non-frisky cat, who is sleeping
on the top bunk where Carli sleeps.

Carli grabs Buttons right out of her dead sleep and gives her a big squeeze. Buttons screams loud for help as Carli gives her all of her love then gives Buttons her Kitty treats and Buttons is happy again and purring sleepily.

Now that Carli is home, Buttons goes to sit in front of the sliding glass door to watch all the animals at play. What's this? Mac is staring at Buttons and scared Buttons into hiding under the end-table. What a scaredy cat!!

Now it's time for Buttons and Carli to play their favorite game: Chase.
The rules of the game is: Buttons chases Carli until Carli laughs so
hard she can't run any more.

Then they begin to play Hide-and-Seek. The rules to this game are simple: Carli hides and Buttons finds her and taps her with her paw
as if to say, "Now you're it!"

Well, it's time for spaghetti dinner with garlic bread. Buttons is back to her bird watching. Although, I don't suspect she really wants to find any birds; especially Mac. But watching Josh and Gosh has always been entertaining for her.

Carli is setting the table for dinner and Buttons sticks her paw out to trip Carli and gives a big laugh because Carli won the Hide-and-Seek game today. We all had a good laugh thanks to Buttons. She is soooo funny!

Everyone sits down to eat Grandma's Italian family feast and had a wonderful dinner together. Even Buttons enjoys Grandma's sauce on her kibbles.

After dinner it seems most of the animals are at rest. Except ... Grandma, do you smell something? Oh yes, Sherry, isn't it amazing! Italian Spaghetti always makes a kitchen smell like a home.

Uh, no Grandma ... it's not the wonderful smell of spaghetti. This smells like ... well, it just SMELLS!!!

Oh no, Grandma, the skunk family is here. Sherry says, "I thought they were just really stinky kittens." Carli says, "Oh Mom, you're unbelievable." Grandma says, "Now what?" Sherry says, "Let's give them some peanut butter and grape jelly and lead them next door to the neighbor's house. I heard grape jelly is their favorite from Trapper John. Grandma says, "That sounds great!"

Getting time to put our pajamas on and watch some television. Let's watch Animal Planet, Yeah! Everyone is helping to make a big bowl of popcorn and sits down ready to watch television and cuddle up for the night with their blankets; even Buttons.

Hey, wait a minute! What's all that noise and where's it coming from. "Grandma, do you hear all of that? "Carli, do you hear that?" Sherry says, "I hear so much rumbling. Is that coming from the roof?" Grandma says, "It's those rascally raccoons up on the roof. There must be at least 10 of them from the sound of it. Five on each side like they're playing hockey or something." Sherry says, "Hey, I'll bet they are playing "Hockey on the Roof!"

THE END

Printed in the United States
by Baker & Taylor Publisher Services